TRUSTING GOD

REDEEMING PROMISES OF THE WORD

TRUSTING GOD

REDEEMING PROMISES OF THE WORD

© 2021 The Rev. Charlie Holt

All rights reserved.

Published in Houston, Texas by Bible Study Media, Inc.

ISBN # 978-1-942243-46-5
Ebook ISBN # 978-1-942243-46-5

Library of Congress Control Number:
2021900144

No part of this publication may be reproduced, stored in retrieval system, or transmitted in any form or by any means electronic, mechanical, photocopy, recording, or otherwise except for brief quotations in printed reviews, without the prior written permission of the publisher. www.biblestudymedia.com.

Unless otherwise indicated, all Scripture quotations are from the ESV® Bible (The Holy Bible, English Standard Version®), copyright © 2001 by Crossway, a publishing ministry of Good News Publishers. Used by permission. All rights reserved.

Printed in the United States of America

TABLE OF CONTENTS

Introduction 6
Using This Study 9
Outline of Each Session 11
Daily Scripture Reading Plan 14

Week One - Adam: The Promise of Abundant Life 17
Week Two - Noah: The Promise of New Beginnings 25
Week Three - Abraham: The Promise of Great Blessing 33
Week Four - Moses: The Promise of Abiding Presence 41
Week Five - David: The Promise of the Forever Kingdom 49
Week Six - Jesus: The Promise of Eternal Life 57

Appendices 66
Small Group Covenant 70
Group Calendar 71
Prayer & Praise Journal 72
Small Group Roster 73

Small Group Leader Helps 75
Leading for the First Time 76
Leadership Training 101 77

INTRODUCTION

The redeeming promises of God afford us with abundant reasons to trust God with his plan for our lives. With this being the case, why is trust so difficult? The entire story of the Bible tells of a God who makes covenantal promises to his people. In response, the call is to trust him.

The Apostle Peter writes in his second letter:

> *"His divine power has granted to us all things that pertain to life and godliness, through the knowledge of him who called us to his own glory and excellence, by which he has granted to us his precious and very great promises, so that through them you may become partakers of the divine nature, having escaped from the corruption that is in the world because of sinful desire."*
>
> 2 PETER 1:3-4

The Lord has given us everything that we need for life in his most excellent Word. The "precious and great promises" offer us a transformational pathway that leads to glorious life with God. And still we struggle with trust!

In *Trusting God: Redeeming Promises of the Word*, we will explore the six major redeeming promises of God found in his Word. They were made to and through individual people, yet they are applicable to all people. Each week we will reflect on a particular promise. The daily reading assignments will help provide a rich context into the promise. Ideally, the videos and study guide will be answered in the context of a small group of fellow Christians, but you can also embark on this journey as a self-study.

The six promises are:

    Adam: The Promise of Abundant Life
    Noah: The Promise of New Beginnings
    Abraham: The Promise of Great Blessing
    Moses: The Promise of Abiding Presence
    David: The Promise of the Forever Kingdom
    Jesus: The Promise of Eternal Life

As you embark on this study as a small group or an individual, I pray that you will marvel in the amazing redeeming promises of God and that your trust in him will grow strong and true. His "precious and great promises" are for you.

I am faithfully yours in Christ Jesus our Lord,

Charlie Holt

Crucifixion, The Way of the Cross, Basilica of Our Lady of Hanswijk, Mechelen, Belgium. 19th Century.

USING THIS STUDY
HOW TO GET THE MOST OUT OF THIS STUDY

As with any individual or small group study of God's Word, you largely reap what you sow—or, as it is commonly put, you get out of it what you put into it. But additionally, there are guidelines that can help you get the most from the efforts you put in. I have outlined some suggestions here for you and your group to review before you get started.

1. Review the Table of Contents. The section entitled "Small Group Leader Helps" lays out best practices for how to host and facilitate a healthy small group and avoid common mistakes. It's a great idea to review this material before having your first meeting.

2. This book is a tool for facilitation. Adapt it to the needs of your group. If a line of discussion leads to green pastures outside the scope of the book, enjoy the leading of the Good Shepherd. Feel free to ask, or allow other members to ask, insightful questions as the Holy Spirit leads.

3. There is a lot of material here. You do not have to ask every question in your group discussion. Feel free to skip questions as needed and linger over the ones where there is authentic conversation.

4. Enjoy the experience. Christian community should be characterized by joy and love. Encourage yourself and the group members to bear such fruit. Pray before each session—ask God

to minister to you, the facilitator, and every group member by name. Pray for the discussion, the fellowship, and the personal application.

5. Read the "Outline of Each Session" on the following pages so you understand the flow of the session and how the study works.

OUTLINE OF EACH SESSION

OPENING AND CLOSING PRAYER

Begin and end each session with prayer. Invite God into the midst of your conversation. Use the prayers provided or offer one of your own. The prayers provided could be offered by a member of the group or you could all say them together. Close your group with an offer to pray with one another. There is a prayer journal on p. 72 where you can keep track of prayer requests and God's answers to your prayers.

KEY VERSE

Each session begins with a key verse. This verse is a key to understanding the entire week's theme. You may want to memorize these verses. By committing portions of God's Word to long-term memory, you will always have them to refer to even when you don't have a Bible with you.

REKINDLE THE PROMISE

As we gather, a couple of questions are offered to rekindle the fire of our faith in God and mutual trust in one another. Use the opening questions as an opportunity to reconnect each week and re-engage in the discussion.

REMEMBER GOD'S PROMISE

Christians leak. As many times as we have heard the precious and great promises of God, we need continual reminding. The video teachings and assigned group Scripture reading are there to help us focus on the promises of the week and hear again of God's covenant love.

The video segment will provide teaching on the passage and direction for the session, serving as a launchpad for your discussion. You can watch this video ahead of the meeting as individuals, or if possible, watch it as a group. If you are hosting this group as an online group and are experiencing diminished quality, you may need to encourage members to take time to watch the video on their own rather than try to play it through your online meeting platform.

The "Video Notes" section offers summaries of key points from the video teaching. You may want to ask the group a simple question after the video, something like: "What resonated with you from that video teaching?"

There will also be a section of Scripture for the group to read aloud. Questions will follow to help group members make observations and interpret the text. Use as many or as few of these questions as prove helpful.

RENEW THE PROMISE

As we hear God's Word together, we are called to respond by being drawn into deeper trust of God and one another. The third section of every study will seek to call your hearts to greater intimacy and vulnerability with God and your brothers and sisters in Christ. The questions in this section will invite you to apply what you are learning through fellowship, prayer, and corporate worship.

The "Study Notes" section provides space to take notes as you watch the video or hear inspirational thoughts from the Lord or from members of your group.

DAILY READINGS

Studying the redeeming promises of the Word is like mining a rich vein of gold. The deeper you dig, the more treasure you will discover. Set aside time to spend with the Lord each day. The Scripture reading assignments will stimulate your personal interaction with God and his Word. Pray and ask the Lord to reveal himself to you through the pages of his Word. Use the space provided to journal what you are hearing and learning from the Lord or to express your prayers and praises.

Moses Strikes Water from the Rock. Niccolò Bambini, Chiesa di San Moiseby. Venice, Italy.

DAILY SCRIPTURE READING PLAN

WEEK ONE - ADAM:
THE PROMISE OF ABUNDANT LIFE

DAY	READING
1	GENESIS 1:1-2:3
2	GENESIS 2:4-25
3	GENESIS 3:1-13
4	GENESIS 3:14-24
5	GENESIS 4:1-26
6	ROMANS 5:12-21
7	REVELATION 22:1-21

WEEK TWO - NOAH:
THE PROMISE OF NEW BEGINNINGS

DAY	READING
8	GENESIS 6:1-22
9	GENESIS 7:1-24
10	GENESIS 8:1-22
11	GENESIS 9:1-29
12	ISAIAH 54:1-17
13	1 PETER 3:8-4:11
14	2 PETER 3:1-18

WEEK THREE - ABRAHAM:
THE PROMISE OF GREAT BLESSING

DAY	READING
15	GENESIS 11:1-9
16	GENESIS 12:1-9
17	GENESIS 15:1-21
18	GENESIS 17:1-27
19	GENESIS 22:1-18
20	ROMANS 4:1-25
21	GALATIANS 3:1-29

WEEK FOUR - MOSES:
THE PROMISE OF ABIDING PRESENCE

DAY	READING
22	EXODUS 3:1-22
23	EXODUS 12:1-28
24	EXODUS 20:1-21
25	DEUTERONOMY 8:1-20
26	DEUTERONOMY 11:1-32
27	DEUTERONOMY 30:1-20
28	HEBREWS 12:1-29

WEEK FIVE - DAVID:
THE PROMISE OF THE FOREVER KINGDOM

DAY	READING
29	2 SAMUEL 7:1-17
30	2 SAMUEL 7:18-29
31	PSALM 2:1-12
32	PSALM 110:1-7, 111:1-10
33	MATTHEW 3:1-17
34	MATTHEW 17:1-13
35	MATTHEW 21:33-46

WEEK SIX - JESUS:
THE PROMISE OF ETERNAL LIFE

DAY	READING
36	ISAIAH 42:1-9
37	ISAIAH 52:13-53:12
38	JEREMIAH 31:23-40
39	EZEKIEL 36:16-38
40	ACTS 2:1-21
41	ACTS 2:22-41
42	HEBREWS 10:1-25

Adam & Eve Eat Forbidden Fruit. Julius Schnorr von Carolsfeld. Die Bibel in Bildern. St. Petersburg Russia, 1860.

WEEK 1

ADAM: THE PROMISE OF ABUNDANT LIFE

Almighty God, whose blessed Son was led by the Spirit to be tempted by Satan: Come quickly to help us who are assaulted by many temptations; and, as you know the weaknesses of each of us, let each one find you mighty to save; through Jesus Christ your Son our Lord, who lives and reigns with you and the Holy Spirit, one God, now and for ever. *Amen.*

BOOK OF COMMON PRAYER, P. 218

KEY VERSE

"I will put enmity between you and the woman, and between your offspring and her offspring; he shall bruise your head, and you shall bruise his heel." - GENESIS 3:15

INTRODUCTION

The first promise to humanity was expansive. Humanity was given abundant and limitless access to any tree in the Garden of Eden. The first man and woman walked with God in the cool of the morning. Abundant life was made available through the incredible gift of the Tree of Life.

Our first parents were warned not to eat of one tree in the garden—the Tree of the Knowledge of Good and Evil. This single stipulation came with a warning:

"The day you eat of it, you will surely die" - GENESIS 2:17

Because of the ignorance of innocence, temptation, and manipulation by Satan, humanity made the choice to forfeit abundant life in exchange for the false promise of intimately knowing good and evil. The image of God was now reflected in a shattered visage. Yet, even in their fall, God made a redeeming promise.

REKINDLE THE PROMISE

1. If you have a new group or new members, take some time to introduce one another and share your hopes for this study.

2. Do you think that most people in our day have trust issues?

3. Do you have a hard time trusting God? Why or why not?

REMEMBER GOD'S PROMISE

Watch the Video

The video teaching can be found at https://biblestudymedia.com/trustinggod. If you are hosting this group as an online group and are experiencing diminished quality, you may need to encourage members to take time to watch the video on their own rather than try to play it through your online meeting platform.

Video Notes

The Creation Mandate:
Humanity was given three charges: to reflect God's image, to fruitfully reproduce his image across the earth, and to rule as faithful stewards over his creation. With the mandate came abundance and blessing. God saw all that he made and called it very good.

The Fall:
The first human parents failed to trust God. While ignorance was bliss, intimacy with sin brought a curse. The fall of humanity into sin had devasting consequences. Humans were banished from the abundance of the Garden of Eden. The Tree of Life was no longer accessible. Their lives would be burdened with toilsome labor and painful childbearing. Guilt and shame caused fear and self-hiding from God. Trust was broken.

The Redeeming Promise:
Yet, God provided redeeming promises that would point the way back to abundant life. First, he covered the shame of Adam and Eve by providing the skins from animals, thus foreshadowing the blood sacrifice of Jesus. Second, God made the first announcement of the Gospel: a redeeming promise that the seed of the woman would crush the head of the serpent. One day the war against evil would be over, and a child of Eve would win the battle.

4. What resonated with you from that video teaching? What was a new insight?

READ SCRIPTURE: GENESIS 1:26-31

5. What do you think it means to reflect God's image? What happens to that reflection when we turn our lives away from God?

6. In verse 1:28, *"God blessed them."* How do you see that blessing made manifest in these verses?

7. How would the fall of humanity into evil impact our stewardship over the creation?

RENEW THE PROMISE

8. Read Genesis 3:15, how would you explain in your own words the redeeming promise of the first Gospel? How does this passage point to Jesus Christ, and what encouragement does this promise give you?

9. The creation mandate has three R's: reflect God's image, reproduce his image, and reign as stewards? Which one of the three R's will become a personal focus for you this week?

10. Jesus said in John 10:10, *"The thief comes only to steal and kill and destroy. I came that they may have life and have it abundantly."* How is this verse manifested in your life today?

PRAYER REQUESTS

You may want to share prayer requests with one another. There's a Prayer & Praise Journal found on p. 72 where you can keep track of your group's requests. Have someone close in prayer or pray the following prayer together:

O God, who wonderfully created, and yet more wonderfully restored, the dignity of human nature: Grant that we may share the divine life of him who humbled himself to share our humanity, your Son Jesus Christ; who lives and reigns with you, in the unity of the Holy Spirit, one God, for ever and ever. Amen.

BOOK OF COMMON PRAYER, P. 252

STUDY NOTES

STUDY NOTES

Noah's Sacrifice and the Rainbow. Julius Schnorr von Carolsfeld. Die Bibel in Bildern, Plate 20, St. Petersburg Russia, 1860.

WEEK 2

NOAH: THE PROMISE OF NEW BEGINNINGS

Almighty and everlasting Father, in your great mercy you saved Noah and his family in the Ark from the destruction of the flood, prefiguring the Sacrament of Holy Baptism. Look mercifully upon us. Thank you for washing and sanctifying us through your Holy Spirit, delivering us from destruction and receiving us into the Ark of Christ's Church; and being steadfast in faith, joyful through hope, and rooted in love, may we pass through the turbulent floods of this troublesome world and come into the land of everlasting life, through Jesus Christ our Lord. *Amen.*

BOOK OF COMMON PRAYER (ANGLICAN, 2019), P. 167

KEY VERSE

"I establish my covenant with you, that never again shall all flesh be cut off by the waters of the flood, and never again shall there be a flood to destroy the earth.' And God said, 'This is the sign of the covenant that I make between me and you and every living creature that is with you, for all future generations: I have set my bow in the cloud, and it shall be a sign of the covenant between me and the earth." - GENESIS 9:11-13

INTRODUCTION

In Sunday School, we learn the children's version of Noah's ark with an emphasis on the boat and the animals. The beloved part of the story is one of a rainbow and a promise. However, the full biblical version does not shield us from the reality that the entire human race had become utterly corrupt in the fall. The Lord's indictment on humanity was sharp and his judgment severe:

"The LORD saw that the wickedness of man was great in the earth, and that every intention of the thoughts of his heart was only evil continually. And the LORD regretted that he had made man on the earth, and it grieved him to his heart. So the LORD said, 'I will blot out man whom I have created from the face of the land, man and animals and creeping things and birds of the heavens, for I am sorry that I have made them.'" - GENESIS 6:5-7

A global flood was an awesome display of God's judgment against evil. Noah and his family were the seeds of a new humanity, when the Lord literally started over from one man, one family. The precious and great promise of the rainbow in the clouds provides stability and confidence for human flourishing. Humanity was given a reset to fulfill the creation mandate to reflect, reproduce, and reign. It was a promise of a new beginning.

REKINDLE THE PROMISE

1. What do you think about when you see a rainbow in the sky?

2. Tell of a moment where you received a second chance or a fresh start.

REMEMBER GOD'S PROMISE

Watch the Video

The video teaching can be found at https://biblestudymedia.com/trustinggod. If you are hosting this group as an online group and are experiencing diminished quality, you may need to encourage members to take time to watch the video on their own rather than try to play it through your online meeting platform.

Video Notes

The Corruption of Humanity:
While being fruitful and multiplying is part of the creation mandate, if humanity is corrupt, then evil is spread instead of good. Prior to the flood, the corruption of man was such that *"every intention of the thoughts of his heart was only evil continually"* (Genesis 6:5). Notice the "every" and the "only"—total depravity.

The Flood:
God would blot out humanity from the face of the earth. This judgment was a type of cleansing. The consequence of sin was death. A sinful human race was condemned to die. Noah and his family were spared. Unfortunately, the seed of sin was still carried within the hearts of Noah and sons, then passed on to the generations that would follow.

The Redeeming Promise:
God hung his rainbow in the cloud. Global corruption of the human race would become an inevitable eventuality. However, the sign of the bow in the clouds was not only a promise to humanity and the creation, but a reminder to God himself that his arrows of judgment were aimed at himself pointing to another ultimate remedy needed to deal with sin—the atonement of the cross.

A New Beginning:
Humanity was given a new beginning. The New Testament would point to the new beginning given in baptism as a fresh start for a life under grace and the salvation of the Lord. In 1 Peter 3:20-21, the waters that saved Noah are compared to our baptism in Christ. Like Noah, we are given a clean slate and renewed "good conscience" in Christ Jesus' death and resurrection.

> 3. What resonated with you from that video teaching? What was a new insight?

READ SCRIPTURE: 2 PETER 3:1-13

> 4. How are the "scoffers" of Jesus' second coming like those who perished in the flood? In what ways do people of the world take for granted the stability given in the promise made to Noah?

> 5. What benefit does the restraint of God's promised final judgment provide for us (See 2 Peter 3:9)?

> 6. How do you understand the phrase in 2 Peter 3:10, *"the day of the Lord will come like a thief"* (See also Matthew 24:36-44)?

RENEW THE PROMISE

"By faith Noah, being warned by God concerning events as yet unseen, in reverent fear constructed an ark for the saving of his household. By this he condemned the world and became an heir of the righteousness that comes by faith." - HEBREWS 11:7

7. Why does this verse commend Noah as a man of trusting faith? How does the example of Noah's "reverent fear" encourage our trust in God's promises?

8. In the video, we learned that waters of baptism signify a clean slate by the cross and resurrection and a new "good conscience" by the indwelling Holy Spirit. How will you embrace and apply your "new beginning" this week?

9. Where do you see your trust in God's promises growing and developing in your mind and heart through this study?

PRAYER REQUESTS

You may want to share prayer requests with one another. There's a Prayer & Praise Journal found on p. 72 where you can keep track of your group's requests. Have someone close in prayer or pray the following prayer together:

Almighty God, we thank you that by the death and resurrection of your Son Jesus Christ you have overcome sin and brought us to yourself, and that by the sealing of your Holy Spirit you have bound us to your service. Renew in us your servants the covenant you made with us at our baptism. Send us forth in the power of the Spirit to perform the service you set before us; through Jesus Christ your Son our Lord, who lives and reigns with you and the Holy Spirit, one God, now and for ever. Amen.

BOOK OF COMMON PRAYER, P. 309

STUDY NOTES

STUDY NOTES

The Sacrifice of Isaac. Julius Schnorr von Carolsfeld. Die Bibel in Bildern. Plate 28, St. Petersburg Russia, 1860

WEEK 3

ABRAHAM: THE PROMISE OF GREAT BLESSING

O God, whose glory it is always to have mercy: Be gracious to all who have gone astray from your ways, and bring them again with penitent hearts and steadfast faith to embrace and hold fast the unchangeable truth of your Word, Jesus Christ your Son; who with you and the Holy Spirit lives and reigns, one God, for ever and ever. Amen.

BOOK OF COMMON PRAYER, P. 289

KEY VERSE

"Now the LORD said to Abram, 'Go from your country and your kindred and your father's house to the land that I will show you. And I will make of you a great nation, and I will bless you and make your name great, so that you will be a blessing. I will bless those who bless you, and him who dishonors you I will curse, and in you all the families of the earth shall be blessed.'" - GENESIS 12:1-3

INTRODUCTION

God alone will be the source of our greatness. We do not make for ourselves a great name. Once again, God would reestablish his plan to give abundant blessings to humanity. God alone is the source of great blessing. The redeeming promises to Abraham reveal God's plan of salvation for all the peoples of the world. God gives seven "I will" promises to Abraham:

- I will give you the land.
- I will make you a great nation.
- I will bless you.
- I will make your name great.
- I will bless those who bless you.
- I will curse those who curse you.
- I will bless all the families of the earth through you.

Abraham is commended as a man who believed and trusted in the promises of God. His faith in the promise was credited to him as righteousness. Through a divinely ordained family named Israel, the chosen seed of Abraham, Isaac, and Jacob would grow to bear the fruit of great blessing for the world.

REKINDLE THE PROMISE

1. What does the word "blessing" mean to you? How would having your name be great be a blessing to you?

2. Do you see God as tight-fisted with his blessings or lavish and abundant?

REMEMBER GOD'S PROMISE

Watch the Video

The video teaching can be found at https://biblestudymedia.com/trustinggod. If you are hosting this group as an online group and are experiencing diminished quality, you may need to encourage members to take time to watch the video on their own rather than try to play it through your online meeting platform.

Video Notes

Doubt:
Humans have a hard time trusting—even God's promises. God reaffirmed his promise to make Abraham a great nation by multiplying his descendants to be as numerous as the stars of heaven. Still, Abraham struggled with unbelief: *"After these things the word of the LORD came to Abram in a vision: 'Fear not, Abram, I am your shield; your reward shall be very great.' But Abram said, 'O Lord GOD, what will you give me, for I continue childless, and the heir of my house is Eliezer of Damascus?'"* (Genesis 15:1-2).

Reassuring Signs:
The Lord knows that we need help to develop trust. One of the main ways that God overcomes our doubts and fears is to provide covenantal signs. The rainbow in the clouds is an example. For Abraham, the sign of the smoking

fire pot passing through the cut animals provided a reassuring sign that God would keep his promise. Like the bow in the clouds, God was again signifying a curse on himself if he failed to keep his promise to Abraham.

The Righteous Faith:

Abraham is commended for his trust in God's promise. Understandably, he struggled with seeing how God could possibly fulfill his word to him when he was an old man with a wife beyond her childbearing years. *"In hope he believed against hope, that he should become the father of many nations, as he had been told, 'So shall your offspring be'"* (Romans 4:18). Abraham's faith was credited to him as righteousness.

3. What resonated with you from that video teaching? What was a new insight?

READ SCRIPTURE: GENESIS 22:1-18

4. How did God test Abraham's faith? Why do you think it was important for Abraham to be willing to sacrifice the child of the promise?

5. What do you think Abraham was thinking as he climbed the mountain with his son (See Hebrews 11:17-19)?

6. What sign did God give that would help Abraham to grow in his trust of God (Genesis 22:13)? What lessons did Abraham learn from this experience (Genesis 22:14)?

RENEW THE PROMISE

7. How does the gift of the substitute ram foreshadow the death of Jesus on the cross?

8. Have you ever had your faith tested to an extreme? What did you experience during the test? What lessons did you learn?

9. Has the Lord ever proven to you that you can trust him? Where have you seen the Lord's provision for your faith through signs and symbols of his redeeming promises?

PRAYER REQUESTS

You may want to share prayer requests with one another. There's a Prayer & Praise Journal found on p. 72 where you can keep track of your group's requests. Have someone close in prayer or pray the following prayer together:

Almighty God, you know that we have no power in ourselves to help ourselves: Keep us both outwardly in our bodies and inwardly in our souls, that we may be defended from all adversities which may happen to the body, and from all evil thoughts which may assault and hurt the soul; through Jesus Christ our Lord, who lives and reigns with you and the Holy Spirit, one God, for ever and ever. Amen.

BOOK OF COMMON PRAYER, P. 218

STUDY NOTES

STUDY NOTES

Moses and the Burning Bush. Artist: Julius Schnorr von Carolsfeld. Die Bibel in Bildern. St. Petersburg, Russia, 1860.

WEEK 4

MOSES: THE PROMISE OF ABIDING PRESENCE

O God, whose wonderful deeds of old shine forth even to our own day, you once delivered by the power of your mighty arm your chosen people from slavery under Pharaoh, to be a sign for us of the salvation of all nations by the water of baptism: Grant that all the peoples of the earth may be numbered among the offspring of Abraham, and rejoice in the inheritance of Israel; through Jesus Christ our Lord. *Amen.*

BOOK OF COMMON PRAYER, P. 289

KEY VERSE

"Say therefore to the people of Israel, 'I am the Lord, and I will bring you out from under the burdens of the Egyptians, and I will deliver you from slavery to them, and I will redeem you with an outstretched arm and with great acts of judgment. I will take you to be my people, and I will be your God, and you shall know that I am the Lord your God, who has brought you out from under the burdens of the Egyptians. I will bring you into the land that I swore to give to Abraham, to Isaac, and to Jacob. I will give it to you for a possession. I am the Lord.'" - EXODUS 6:6-8

INTRODUCTION

The cruel bondage experienced by the Israelites suffering in Egypt made it difficult for them to believe the promises uttered by Moses. In Exodus 6:9 we read, *"Moses spoke thus to the people of Israel, but they did not listen to Moses, because of their broken spirit and harsh slavery."* The Lord would demonstrate his covenantal love for his people by rescuing and redeeming them from slavery like a warrior husband rescues his bride in distress, or like a father would redeem a son.

Central to the covenant with Moses is a promise of God's abiding presence, which was gloriously manifested in the tent of meeting and the ark of the covenant. Moses would experience God's presence in a burning bush, on a holy mountain, and in a tent of meeting. The promises of God were always connected to the abiding presence of God.

The Israelites would learn that drawing near to the Lord's abiding presence required faithful obedience to the commandments of God. Holiness of life led to blessing with the Lord's presence in the promised land. But disobedience would forfeit the promises and result in costly consequences and exile from the Lord. Trusting God's commandments was hard for the people living in a corrupt and idolatrous world.

REKINDLE THE PROMISE

1. Why does suffering make it difficult to trust God?

2. Do you find it difficult or easy to trust and obey the Lord's commands and way of life?

REMEMBER GOD'S PROMISE

Watch the Video

The video teaching can be found at https://biblestudymedia.com/trustinggod. If you are hosting this group as an online group and are experiencing diminished quality, you may need to encourage members to take time to watch the video on their own rather than try to play it through your online meeting platform.

Video Notes

Redemption:
The Lord would do anything for his beloved people. The rescue of the Israelites from Egypt by signs and wonders was a powerful demonstration of God's covenant love and commitment to his Word.

The Two Tablets:
The redeeming promises made through Moses came with the law of God. The commands were literally written in stone by the finger of God. With the giving of the law, God revealed his plan to dwell in the midst of his people. The law provided the instructions on how the Israelites could remain in his holy presence and live without fear or shame.

Blessings and Curses:
Israel learned to trust and obey God's word of promise the hard way. They pushed and pulled against God's salvation with grumbling and overt acts of rebellion. Yet, the Lord demonstrated time and time again that while he

would discipline sin and rebellion, his nature is overwhelmingly manifested in love, forgiveness, and blessing.

3. What resonated with you from that video teaching? What was a new insight?

READ SCRIPTURE: DEUTERONOMY 30:1-20

4. What do see as the central promise of Deuteronomy 30?

5. How hard was it for the Israelites to know God's will for their lives? How hard is it for us (Deuteronomy 30:11-14, see also Romans 10:5-11)?

6. What were the blessings for obedience? And what were the curses for disobedience?

RENEW THE PROMISE

7. Why is it so important to obey the Lord's will and commands if we want to abide in his presence?

8. How do you experience the bread of communion as Jesus' abiding presence in your life? Where else do you sense his presence?

9. What practical application will you make this week to *"choose life that you might live"*?

PRAYER REQUESTS

You may want to share prayer requests with one another. There's a Prayer & Praise Journal found on p. 72 where you can keep track of your group's requests. Have someone close in prayer or pray the following prayer together:

Gracious Father, whose blessed Son Jesus Christ came down from heaven to be the true bread which gives life to the world: Evermore give us this bread, that he may live in us, and we in him; who lives and reigns with you and the Holy Spirit, one God, now and for ever. Amen.

BOOK OF COMMON PRAYER, P. 219

Egypt. Mount Sinai in the morning at sunrise. (Mount Horeb, Gabal Musa, Moses Mount).

STUDY NOTES

STUDY NOTES

David the Psalmist - Worship. Julius Schnorr von Carolsfeld. Die Bibel in Bildern, Plate 131. St. Petersburg, Russia, 1860.

WEEK 5

DAVID: THE PROMISE OF THE FOREVER KINGDOM

Almighty God, you alone can bring into order the unruly wills and affections of sinners: Grant your people grace to love what you command and desire what you promise; that, among the swift and varied changes of the world, our hearts may surely there be fixed where true joys are to be found; through Jesus Christ our Lord, who lives and reigns with you and the Holy Spirit, one God, now and for ever. *Amen.*

BOOK OF COMMON PRAYER, P. 219

KEY VERSE

"When your days are fulfilled and you lie down with your fathers, I will raise up your offspring after you, who shall come from your body, and I will establish his kingdom. He shall build a house for my name, and I will establish the throne of his kingdom forever. I will be to him a father, and he shall be to me a son. When he commits iniquity, I will discipline him with the rod of men, with the stripes of the sons of men, but my steadfast love will not depart from him, as I took it from Saul, whom I put away from before you. And your house and your kingdom shall be made sure forever before me. Your throne shall be established forever." - 2 SAMUEL 7:12-16

INTRODUCTION

For all his sinful and violent acts, the one thing that can be said for King David is that he loved the Lord. As he experienced peace in his reign and rest from his enemies, David went into a building mode. He realized that while he had a beautiful palace made of cedar, the Lord was still dwelling in the temporary tabernacle.

David purposed in his heart to build a glorious temple for the Lord in the capital city of Jerusalem. However, the Lord would not allow David to be the temple-building king. Instead, he made incredible promises to David.

David's heir would be the one to build a house for the Lord. Moreover, David's son would be called "Son of God," and his kingdom would be established forever. God would build David a house!

REKINDLE THE PROMISE

1. How important is your home to you? What blessings does it provide to you?

2. What do you think God's eternal home will be like?

REMEMBER GOD'S PROMISE

Watch the Video

The video teaching can be found at https://biblestudymedia.com/trustinggod. If you are hosting this group as an online group and are experiencing diminished quality, you may need to encourage members to take time to watch the video on their own rather than try to play it through your online meeting platform.

Video Notes

Son of God:
The heart of the Davidic covenant is an incredible promise that the heir of David's throne would be called God's Son. Psalm 2 was a testimony that the king of Israel is ordained by God to be heir of the entire world.

House of the Lord:
The temple of Solomon would be described as one of the seven wonders of the ancient world. Scripture would proclaim that the physical temple made of stones would be superseded by a living temple, not made with human hands but made with human beings filled with the abiding presence of the living God.

Forever Kingdom:
Just as the earthly temple in Jerusalem would be destroyed, the kingdom of Israel would divide and be conquered because of Israel's and Judah's rebellion. But God's promise to David of the forever kingdom would find its "Yes" with the arrival of Jesus.

Believe the Good News:
As Jesus inaugurated the forever kingdom, he challenged: *"The time is fulfilled, and the kingdom of God is at hand; repent and believe in the gospel"* (Mark 1:15).

Trusting God involves turning our hearts and lives over to the Lord.

3. What resonated with you from that video teaching? What was a new insight?

READ SCRIPTURE: 2 SAMUEL 7:18-29

4. How did David respond to God's redeeming promise to bless his royal line and build him the forever kingdom (v. 18-22)?

5. Why do you think David asked God to *"confirm forever the word that you have spoken"* (v. 25)?

6. Have you ever heard the expression *"claim the promise"*? How is David courageously claiming God's promise?

RENEW THE PROMISE

7. Where do you find it challenging to submit to Jesus as your king and leader?

8. Where do you see tension between living for the kingdoms of this world and living for the forever kingdom?

9. This week, what are you feeling called to surrender and entrust to the lordship of Jesus Christ?

PRAYER REQUESTS

You may want to share prayer requests with one another. There's a Prayer & Praise Journal found on p. 72 where you can keep track of your group's requests. Have someone close in prayer or pray the following prayer together:

Almighty and everlasting God, whose will it is to restore all things in your well-beloved Son, the King of kings and Lord of lords: Mercifully grant that the peoples of the earth, divided and enslaved by sin, may be freed and brought together under his most gracious rule; who lives and reigns with you and the Holy Spirit, one God, now and for ever. Amen.

BOOK OF COMMON PRAYER, P. 236

Mount Sinai, Mount Moses in Egypt. Africa.

STUDY NOTES

STUDY NOTES

The Revelation to St John. Julius Schnorr von Carolsfeld. Die Bibel in Bildern. St. Petersburg Russia, 1860.

WEEK 6

JESUS: THE PROMISE OF ETERNAL LIFE

Almighty and everliving God, in your tender love for the human race you sent your Son our Savior Jesus Christ to take upon him our nature, and to suffer death upon the cross, giving us the example of his great humility: Mercifully grant that we may walk in the way of his suffering, and also share in his resurrection; through Jesus Christ our Lord, who lives and reigns with you and the Holy Spirit, one God, for ever and ever. *Amen.*

BOOK OF COMMON PRAYER, P. 219

KEY VERSE

"For God so loved the world, that he gave his only Son, that whoever believes in him should not perish but have eternal life. For God did not send his Son into the world to condemn the world, but in order that the world might be saved through him." - JOHN 3:16-17

INTRODUCTION

The great mystery of the redeeming promises of God was revealed finally and climactically in the person and work of Jesus. As the Apostle Paul writes in his second letter to the church in Corinth:

"For all the promises of God find their Yes in him. That is why it is through him that we utter our Amen to God for his glory. And it is God who establishes us with you in Christ, and has anointed us, and who has also put his seal on us and given us his Spirit in our hearts as a guarantee." - 2 CORINTHIANS 1:20-22

Jesus fulfills all of God's promises to the people of God and expands them to all the people of this world. The vision of God is that all people would be united under one head in Christ. When the image of God is restored in us, then fruitful multiplication manifests blessing in our stewardship of creation. In Christ, God is reconciling the world to himself, and we have the high and holy privilege of sharing in that promise.

REKINDLE THE PROMISE

1. How does it feel when someone you care about does not keep their promise?

2. Do you see God as One who has kept all of his promises?

REMEMBER GOD'S PROMISE

Watch the Video

The video teaching can be found at https://biblestudymedia.com/trustinggod. If you are hosting this group as an online group and are experiencing diminished quality, you may need to encourage members to take time to watch the video on their own rather than try to play it through your online meeting platform.

Video Notes

Forgiveness of Sin:
The new covenant redeeming promise is one of forgiveness of sin and spiritual resurrection. The written laws of Moses would serve to condemn rather than bless as Israel failed to uphold them. The blood of bulls and goats never could take away the guilt and shame of sin. Israel (and all humanity by extension) desperately needed a Savior—the One who would crush the head of the serpent forever. The cross of Jesus provides the atoning sacrifice for sins once and for all.

The New Heart:
The gift of the Holy Spirit is central to the new covenant. By the Spirit, God writes his laws on our hearts, empowering faithfulness from within. The Lord graciously gives his presence to all who believe in him, thus granting a new beginning and a renewed promise of eternal, abundant life. The Spirit of God given in Christ guarantees the new covenant. The same Spirit that raised Jesus from the dead seals our hearts in Christ for the day when we will receive the promise of eternal life in full.

> 3. What resonated with you from that video teaching? What was a new insight?

READ SCRIPTURE: HEBREWS 10:19-39

4. Why does the "blood of Jesus" and the "sprinkled hearts" of the Spirit give us confidence to enter into the holy place of God's abiding presence (v. 19-22)?

5. Reflecting on Hebrews 10:19-25, which of the many practical responses of trust in the promises resonates with you the most? List the various responses.

6. Why is "sinning deliberately" after receiving the promises such a concern to the Lord (v. 26-31)?

RENEW THE PROMISE

7. In Hebrews 10:32-39, the writer reminds them of their steadfast trust in God during the hard times of persecution. Do you find it harder to trust God in the times of struggle or in the times of plenty and blessing?

8. What have you learned in this study about Trusting God that has impacted you the most?

9. What is your most significant resolution of faith that you are going to make in response to God's redeeming promises?

PRAYER REQUESTS

You may want to share prayer requests with one another. There's a Prayer & Praise Journal found on p. 72 where you can keep track of your group's requests. Have someone close in prayer or pray the following prayer together:

O God, you have made of one blood all the peoples of the earth, and sent your blessed Son to preach peace to those who are far off and to those who are near: Grant that people everywhere may seek after you and find you, bring the nations into your fold, pour out your Spirit upon all flesh, and hasten the coming of your kingdom; through Jesus Christ our Lord, who lives and reigns with you and the Holy Spirit, one God, now and for ever. Amen.

BOOK OF COMMON PRAYER, P. 257

Mount Sinai, Mount Moses in Egypt.

STUDY NOTES

STUDY NOTES

God giving instructions how tho build the ark to Noah and his family, graphic collage from engraving of Nazarene School, published in The Holy Bible, St. Vojtech Publishing, Trnava, Slovakia, 1937.

Moses receiving the ten commandments from God, graphic collage from engraving of Nazarene School, published in The Holy Bible, St. Vojtech Publishing, Trnava, Slovakia, 1937.

APPENDICES

FREQUENTLY ASKED QUESTIONS

WHAT DO WE DO ON THE FIRST NIGHT OF OUR GROUP?

Have a party! A "get to know you" coffee, dinner, or dessert is a great way to launch a new study. You may want to review the Small Group Covenant (page 70) and share the names of a few friends you can invite to join you. But most importantly, have fun before your study time begins.

WHERE DO WE FIND NEW MEMBERS FOR OUR GROUP?

Finding members can be troubling, especially for new groups that have only a few people or for existing groups that have lost a few people along the way. We encourage you to pray with your group and then brainstorm a list of people from work, church, your neighborhood, your children's school, family, the gym, and so forth. Use the five circles on the next page to identify potential group members with whom you would like to build a spiritual friendship. Have each group member invite several of the people on his or her list.

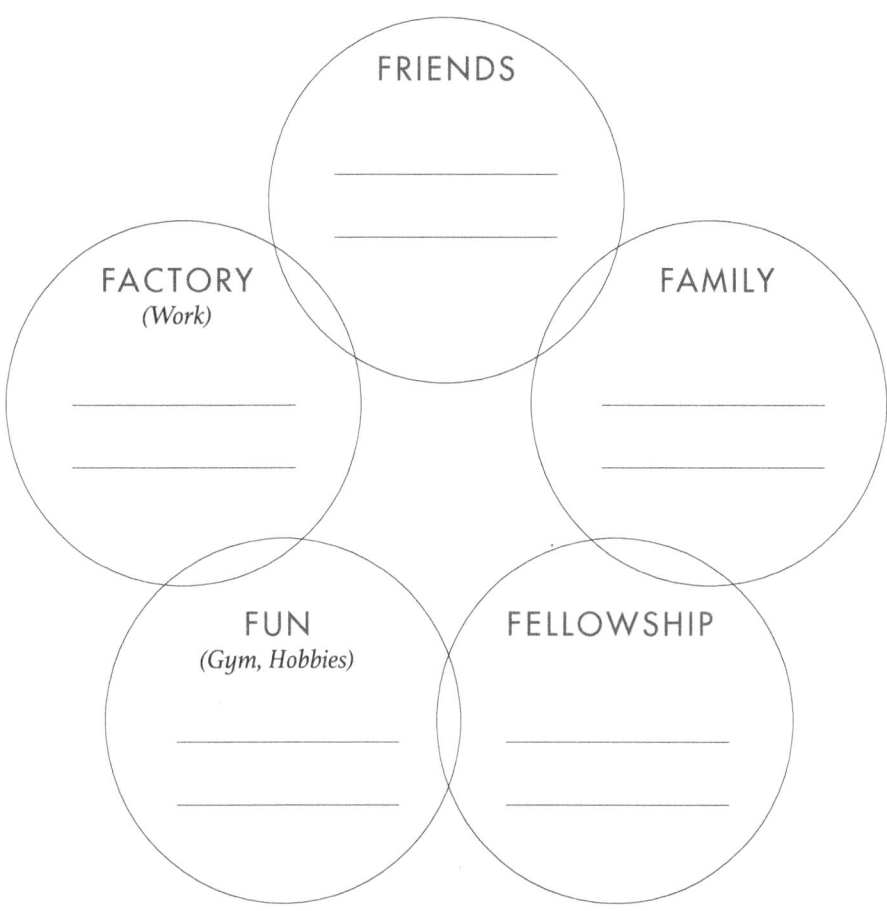

No matter how you find members, it's vital that you stay on the lookout for new people to join your group. All groups tend to go through healthy attrition—the result of moves, sending out new leaders, ministry opportunities, and so forth—and if the group gets too small, it could be at risk of ending. If you and your group stay open to ideas, you'll be amazed at the people God sends your way. The next person just might become a friend for life. You never know!

HOW LONG WILL THIS GROUP MEET?

Most groups meet weekly for at least their first six weeks, but every other week can work as well. We strongly recommend that the group meet for the first six months on a weekly basis if at all possible. This allows for continuity and, if people miss a meeting, they aren't gone for a whole month.

At the end of this study, each group member may decide if he or she wants to continue on for another study. Some groups launch relationships for years to come, and others are stepping-stones into another group experience. Either way, enjoy the journey.

CAN WE DO THIS STUDY ON OUR OWN?

Absolutely! This may sound crazy, but one of the best ways to do this study is not with a full house but with a few friends. You may choose to gather with another couple who would enjoy some relational time (perhaps having a nice dinner) and then walking through this six week study. Jesus will be with you even if there are only two of you (Matthew 18:20).

Estimated location of Noah's Ark in Eastern Turkey, Agri Province.

WHAT IF THIS GROUP IS NOT WORKING FOR US?

You're not alone! This could be the result of a personality conflict, life stage difference, geographical distance, level of spiritual maturity, or any number of things. Relax. Pray for God's direction, and at the end of this six week study, decide whether to continue with this group or find another. You don't typically buy the first car you test drive or marry the first person you date, and the same goes with a group. However, don't bail out before the six weeks are up—God might have something to teach you. Also, don't run from conflict or prejudge people before you have given them a chance. God is still working in your life, too!

WHO IS THE LEADER?

Most groups have an official leader. But ideally, the group will mature, and members will rotate the leadership of meetings. We have discovered that healthy groups rotate hosts/leaders and homes on a regular basis. This model ensures that all members grow, make their unique contribution, and develop their gifts. This study guide and the Holy Spirit can keep things on track even when you rotate leaders. Christ has promised to be in your midst as you gather. Ultimately, God is your leader each step of the way.

HOW DO WE HANDLE THE CHILDCARE NEEDS IN OUR GROUP?

Very carefully. This can be a sensitive issue. We suggest that you empower the group to openly brainstorm solutions. You may try one option that works for a while and then adjust over time. Our favorite approach is for adults to meet in the living room or dining room and to share the cost of a babysitter (or two) who can watch the children in a different part of the house. This way, parents don't have to be away from their children all evening when their children are too young to be left at home. A second option is to use one home for the children and a second home (close by or a phone call away) for the adults. A third idea is to rotate the responsibility of providing a lesson or care for the children either in the same home or in another home nearby. This can be an incredible blessing for young ones. Finally, the most common solution is to decide that you need to have a night to invest in your spiritual lives individually or as a couple and to make your own arrangements for childcare. No matter what decision the group makes, the best approach is to dialogue openly about both the need and the solution.

SMALL GROUP COVENANT

OUR PURPOSE
To provide a predictable environment where participants experience authentic Christian community to grow spiritually.

GROUP ATTENDANCE
To give priority to the group meeting. We will call or email if we will be late or absent. (Completing the Group Calendar on the next page will minimize this issue.)

SAFE ENVIRONMENT
To help create a safe place where people can be heard and feel loved. (Please, no quick answers, snap judgments, or simple fixes.)

RESPECT DIFFERENCES
To be gentle and gracious with different spiritual maturity levels, personal opinions, temperaments, or "imperfections" in fellow group members. We are all works in progress.

CONFIDENTIALITY
To keep anything that is shared strictly confidential and within the group, and to avoid sharing improper information about those outside the group.

SHARED OWNERSHIP
To remember that every member is a minister and to ensure that each attender will share a small team role or responsibility over time.

ROTATING HOSTS, FACILITATORS, AND HOMES
To encourage different people to host the group in their homes and to rotate the responsibility of facilitating each meeting.

GROUP CALENDAR

Planning and calendaring can help ensure the greatest participation at every meeting. At the end of each meeting, review this calendar. Be sure to include a regular rotation of host homes and facilitator, and don't forget birthdays, socials, church events, holidays, and mission/ministry projects.

DATE	SESSION	HOST HOME	SNACKS	FACILITATOR
	1			
	2			
	3			
	4			
	5			
	6			

PRAYER & PRAISE JOURNAL

SESSION 1
_____
_____

SESSION 2
_____
_____

SESSION 3
_____
_____

SESSION 4
_____
_____

SESSION 5
_____
_____

SESSION 6
_____
_____

SMALL GROUP ROSTER

NAME	EMAIL	PHONE

Icon of The Crossing of the Red Sea – Moses leading Israelites through the Sea of Reeds. The Greek Catholic Church of Saint Elijah. Sečovská Polianka, Slovakia

SMALL GROUP LEADER HELPS

HOSTING AN OPEN HOUSE

If you're starting a new group, try planning an Open House before your first formal group meeting. Even if you have only two to four core members, it's a great way to break the ice and prayerfully consider who else might be open to joining you over the next few weeks. You can also use this kick-off meeting to hand out books, spend some time getting to know each other, discuss each person's expectations for the group, and briefly pray for each other. A simple meal or good dessert always make a kick-off meeting more fun. After people introduce themselves and share how they ended up being at the meeting (you can play a game to see who has the wildest story!), have everyone respond to a few icebreaker questions, such as:

- What is your favorite family vacation?
- What is one thing you love about your church/our community?
- What are two things about your life growing up that most people here don't know?

Next, ask everyone to tell what he or she hopes to get out of the study. You might want to review the Small Group Covenant on page 70 and talk about each person's expectations and priorities. Finally, set an open chair (maybe two) in the center of your group and explain that it represents someone who would enjoy or benefit from this group who isn't here yet.

Ask people to pray about inviting someone to join the group over the next few weeks. Hand out postcards and have everyone write an invitation or two. Don't worry about ending up with too many people; you can always have one discussion circle in the living room and another in the dining room after you watch the lesson. Each group could then report prayer requests and progress at the end of the session.

You can skip this kick-off meeting if your time is limited, but you'll experience a huge benefit if you take the time to connect with one another in this way.

LEADING FOR THE FIRST TIME
SEVEN COMMON LEADERSHIP EXPERIENCES. WELCOME TO LIFE OUT IN FRONT!

- Sweaty palms are a healthy sign. The Bible says God is gracious to the humble. Remember who is in control; the time to worry is when you're not worried. Those who are soft in heart (and sweaty-palmed) are those whom God is sure to speak through.

- Seek support. Ask your leader, co-leader, or a close friend to pray for you and prepare with you before the session. Walking through the study will help you anticipate potentially difficult questions and discussion topics.

- Bring your uniqueness to the study. Lean into who you are and how God wants you to uniquely lead the study.

- Prepare. Prepare. Prepare. Go through the session, read the section of Scripture. If you are using the video, listen to the teaching segment. Consider writing in a journal or praying through the day to prepare yourself for what God wants to do. Don't wait until the last minute to prepare.

• Ask for feedback so you can grow. Perhaps in an email or on index cards handed out at the study, have everyone write down three things you did well and one thing you could improve on. Don't get defensive. Instead, show an openness to learn and grow.

• Share with your group what God is doing in your heart. God is searching for those whose hearts are fully his. Share your trials and victories. We promise that people will relate.

• Prayerfully consider whom you would like to pass the baton to next week. It's only fair. God is ready for the next member of your group to go on the faith journey you just traveled. Make it fun and expect God to do the rest.

LEADERSHIP TRAINING 101

Congratulations! You have responded to the call to help shepherd Jesus' flock. There are few other tasks in the family of God that surpass the contribution you will be making. As you prepare to lead, whether it is one session or the entire series, here are a few thoughts to keep in mind. We encourage you to read these and review them with each new discussion leader before he or she leads.

1. Remember that you are not alone. God knows everything about you, and he knew that you would be asked to lead this group. Remember that it is common for all good leaders to feel that they are not ready to lead. Moses, Solomon, Jeremiah, and Timothy were all reluctant to lead. God promises, *"Never will I leave you; never will I forsake you"* (Hebrews 13:5). Whether you

are leading for one evening, for several weeks, or for a lifetime, you will be blessed as you serve.

2. Don't try to do it alone. Pray right now for God to help you build a healthy leadership team. If you can enlist a co-leader to help you lead the group, you will find your experience to be much richer. This is your chance to involve as many people as you can in building a healthy group. All you have to do is call and ask people to help. You'll probably be surprised at the response.

Jesus meets the women of Jerusalem. Fresco in Sint-Joriskerk, or St. George Church, Amersfoort, Netherlands. 19th Century

3. Just be yourself. If you won't be you, who will? God wants you to use your unique gifts and temperament. Don't try to do things exactly like another leader; do them in a way that fits you! Just admit it when you don't have an answer and apologize when you make a mistake. Your group will love you for it, and you'll sleep better at night!

4. Prepare for your meeting ahead of time. Review the session and write down your responses to each question. Pay special attention to exercises that ask group members to do something other than engage in discussion, like take an action. These exercises will help your group live what the Bible teaches, not just talk about it.

5. Pray for your group members by name. Before you begin your session, go around the room in your mind and pray for each member. Ask God to use

your time together to touch the heart of every person uniquely. Expect God to lead you to whomever he wants you to encourage or challenge in a special way. If you listen, God will surely lead!

6. When you ask a question, be patient. Someone will eventually respond. Sometimes people need a moment or two of silence to think about the question. Keep in mind, if silence doesn't bother you, it won't bother anyone else. After someone responds, affirm the response with a simple "thanks" or "good job." Then ask, "How about somebody else?" or "Would someone who hasn't shared like to add anything?" Be sensitive to new people or members who aren't ready to say, pray, or do anything. If you give them a safe setting, they will blossom over time.

7. Provide transitions between questions. When guiding the discussion, always read aloud the transitional paragraphs and the questions. Ask the group if anyone would like to read the paragraphs or Bible passages. Don't call on anyone, but ask for volunteers; then, be patient until someone begins. Be sure to thank the people who read aloud.

8. Break up into small groups each week or a larger group won't stay. If your group has a lot of people, we strongly encourage you to have the group gather sometimes in discussion circles of three or four people during the Rekindle the Promise or Renew the Promise sections of the study. With a greater opportunity to talk in small circles, people will connect more with the study, apply more quickly what they're learning, and ultimately get more out of it. A small circle also encourages a quiet person to participate and tends to minimize the effect of a more dominant or vocal member. It can also help people feel more loved in your group.

When you gather again at the end of the section, you can have one person summarize the highlights from each circle. Small circles are also helpful during prayer time. People who are not accustomed to praying aloud will feel more comfortable trying it with just two or three others.

Also, prayer requests won't take as much time, so circles will have more time to actually pray. When you gather back with the whole group, you can have one person from each circle briefly update everyone on the prayer requests. People are more willing to break into small circles to pray if they know the whole group will hear all the prayer requests.

9. Rotate facilitators weekly. At the end of each meeting, ask the group who should lead the following week. Let the group help select your weekly facilitator. You may be perfectly capable of leading each time, but you will help others grow in their faith and gifts if you give them opportunities to lead. You can use the Group Calendar (p. 71) to fill in the names of the different leaders for all the meetings if you prefer.

10. One final challenge (for new or first-time leaders): Before your first opportunity to lead, look up each of the five passages listed below. Read each one as a devotional exercise to help equip yourself with a shepherd's heart. Trust us on this one. If you do this, you will be more than ready to lead your first meeting.

Matthew 9:36
1 Peter 5:2-4
Psalm 23
Ezekiel 34:11-16
1 Thessalonians 2:7-8, 11-12

NOTES

NOTES

Moses Views Promised Land. Julius Schnorr von Carolsfeld, Sacred Biblical History of the Old and New Testament. Ed. 3. St. Petersburg, Russia, 1873.

www.ingramcontent.com/pod-product-compliance
Lightning Source LLC
Chambersburg PA
CBHW041131110526
44592CB00020B/2766